Italics Print Handwriting For Kids

with Downunder Classics

Italics Print Handwriting for Kids with Downunder Classics

Simple copywork to help your child write beautifully and improve vocabulary while enjoying iconic Australian and New Zealand literature

By Michelle Morrow

Paperback Edition

©2024

ISBN: 978-1-7635287-8-9

Published by My Homeschool

The publishers would like to thank all the contributors to this educational book who have allowed their material to be reproduced.
Our special thanks go to John Greatorex at School Fonts for use of his Foundation Style fonts.
To contact School Fonts the website is:
 www.schoolfonts.com.au
PO Box 40743, Casuarina, NT, 0811.
Telephone 08 89483443 or fax 08 89480783.

Excerpts used in this book are attributed to the author. Many are in the public domain.

This book is copyright. Apart from any fair dealing for the purposes of private study, research, criticism or review as permitted under the Copyright Act, no part may be reproduced, stored in a retrieval system, or transmitted, in any form or by any means, electronic, mechanical, photocopying, recording or otherwise without prior permission.

The authors have made every reasonable effort to attribute authorship. Where this has not occurred, authors or owners are invited to contact the book authors or the publisher.

All enquiries to My Homeschool PTY LTD

https://myhomeschool.com

ABOUT THIS BOOK

Educate your child with this collection of carefully selected Australian and New Zealand literature that is inspiring, encouraging, and uplifting. This printing workbook offers a delightful blend of storytelling and skill building, making the art of handwriting an engaging adventure.

Embark on a literary journey Downunder whilst encouraging excellent penmanship.

COPYWORK

Practise handwriting with copywork—not composition! After a child has been taught a basic handwriting technique they need to improve their handwriting skills. How can they do that? The simple answer is with lots and lots of copywork.

Handwriting practise consists of *copying—not creating!* Remember that composition requires students to focus on content, organisation, spelling and punctuation. If handwriting perfection is also required, the frustration may be overwhelming, leading a child to avoid writing altogether.

During these formative years, the child will gradually become more adept at remembering what the letters look like and how they are formed; continued copywork reinforces this. After a time, a child will become more confident and begin introducing variations or deviations from the copybook form. This is the beginning of their own handwriting style.

Copywork is simply writing out by hand or copying from other written texts or models. This practice has been employed for centuries as a technique for teaching writing skills to young and old scholars. The primary use of copy work is for penmanship—to develop good technical skills.

This resource is simple to use. All your child needs to do is copy the excerpts provided into the blank sections below each line of writing. The italics print font used in the excerpts is a model for them to copy. The aim is for the child to form their letter with precision and care. You can encourage one excerpt a day, or one page a day, but make sure to require neat careful work. Practise makes perfect.

LITERATURE USED IN THIS BOOK

The copywork in this book is gathered from a selection of Australian and New Zealand fiction, poetry, songs, biographies, and nature study. Hopefully, we will introduce your child to some inspiring educational literature. Many of the books are no longer in print but with a little bit of hunting you can often find them online or at a library.

Some of the excerpts chosen use punctuation and vocabulary from another time. In many cases we have changed the punctuation to reflect modern conventions, but in most cases, we have kept the original words used by the authors. Some vocabulary may need further explanation, so please take this opportunity to explain the evolution of language over time. In the poetry excerpts, we have not left a space in between stanzas.

EXCEPTS USED IN THIS BOOK

- Adapted from G H Gibson (1846-1921) *Iron Bark Splinters*
- C J Dennis (1876-1938) from *A Book for Kids*
- Chris Fry from *Nardika Learns to Make a Spear* ©2001
- Lynley Dodd from *Hairy Maclary from Donaldson's Dairy* ©1985
- Lynley Dodd from *Cats Whiskers; Four Favourite Lynley Dodd Stories* ©2003
- D H Souter (1862-1935) from *The Clever Rabbit*
- Janet Martin from by *Noah the Moah* ©2012
- T Bracken (1843-1898) from *God Defend New Zealand*
- Anonymous Bound for *Botany Bay*
- Banjo Patterson (1864-1941) from *Old Man Platypus*
- Nuri Mass (1918-1993) from *The Wonderland of Nature* ©1964
- Katherine Langloh Parker (1856-1940) from *Australian Legendary Tales*
- Amy Mack (1876-1939) from *Bushland Stories*

- Anonymous *Click Go the Shears*

- Adaptation from Jeannie Gunn (1870-1961) *The Little Black Princess*

- Dorothy Wall (1894-1942) from I

- Esther Glen (1881-1940) from *Six Little New Zealanders*

- Colin Thiele (1920-2006) from *Farmer Shultz's Ducks* ©1986

- C J Dennis (1876-1938) from *A Morning Song*

- Author unknown *About Bradman* published 1931

- Mary Malbunka from *When I Was Little Like You* © 2003

- Fiona Doyle from *On Country: Stories by Nyrlotte* © 2006

- Gary Crew from *Bright Star* © 1996

- Sandra Morris from *A New Zealand Nature Journal* ©2014

- Launcelot Harrison ((1880-1928) from *Tails and Tarradiddles*

Coral Island and the Southern Sea

Little chords and octaves

Little flats and sharps,

Make the tunes of angels

Play on golden harps.

Little tiny insects,

Adapted from G H Gibson (1846-1921) from *Iron Bark Splinters*

Coral Island and the Southern Sea

Smaller than a flea,

Make the coral island

In the southern sea.

Little drops of water,

Little grains of sand,

Adapted from G H Gibson (1846-1921) from *Iron Bark Splinters*

Coral Island and the Southern Sea

Make the mighty ocean

And the southern land.

Adapted from G H Gibson (1846-1921) from *Iron Bark Splinters*

Hey, there! Hoop-la!

Hey, there! Hoop-la!

The circus is in town!

Have you seen the elephant?

Have you seen the clown?

Have you seen the acrobats

C J Dennis (1876-1938) from *A Book for Kids*

Hey, there! Hoop-la!

on the dizzy swing?

Have you seen the tumbling

men tumble up and down?

Hoop-la! Hoop-la! The

circus is in town!

C J Dennis (1876-1938) from *A Book for Kids*

Hey, there! Hoop-la!

Hey there! Hoop-la!

Here's the circus troupe!

Here's the educated dog,

jumping through the hoop.

See the Lady Blondin

C J Dennis (1876-1938) from *A Book for Kids*

Hey, there! Hoop-la!

with the parasol and fan.

The lad upon the ladder and

the indian-rubber man.

See the joyful juggler and

the boy who loops the loop.

C J Dennis (1876-1938) from *A Book for Kids*

Hey, there! Hoop-la!

Hey! Hey! Hey! Hey!

Here's the circus troupe!

C J Dennis (1876-1938) from *A Book for Kids*

Growing Up

Little Tommy Tadpole

began to weep and wail,

For little Tommy Tadpole

had lost his little tail.

And his mother didn't

C J Dennis (1876-1938) from *A Book for Kids*

Growing Up

know him as he wept upon

a log.

For he wasn't Tommy Tadpole,

But Mr Thomas Frog.

C J Dennis (1876-1938) from *A Book for Kids*

Nardika Catches A Fish

At first Nardika thought he

was seeing things, but when he

looked again in the surf he

could see the shaft of his spear

shaking with vibrations. At that

Chris Fry from *Nardika Learns to Make a Spear* ©2001

Nardika Catches A Fish

first instant he knew he'd
caught a fish. He was so
thrilled that he was trembling.
He rushed in and pulled the
spear out of the water.

Chris Fry from *Nardika Learns to Make a Spear* ©2001

Hairy Maclary

Out of the gate,

and off for a walk,

went Hairy Maclary

from Donaldson's Dairy.

With tails in the air

L. Dodd from *Hairy Maclary from Donaldson's Dairy* ©1985

Hairy Maclary

they trotted on down,

past the shops and the park

to the far end of town.

L. Dodd from *Hairy Maclary from Donaldson's Dairy* ©1985

Slinky Malinki

The house was asleep.

It was silent and still,

with flickering shadows

on ceiling and sill.

Slinky Malinki

L Dodd from *Cats Whiskers; Four Favourite Lynley Dodd Stories* ©2003

Slinky Malinki

was cosy and snug,

curled in a ball

on a raggedy rug.

L Dodd from *Cats Whiskers; Four Favourite Lynley Dodd Stories* ©2003

The Clever Rabbit

There was a little rabbit,

Who was lying in his

burrow,

When a dingo rang him

up to say,

D H Souter (1862-1935) from *The Clever Rabbit*

The Clever Rabbit

He'd call on him tomorrow...

But the rabbit thought it

better

That the dingo didn't meet

him.

D H Souter (1862-1935) from *The Clever Rabbit*

The Clever Rabbit

So he found another burrow

And the dingo didn't eat him.

D H Souter (1862-1935) from *The Clever Rabbit*

Noah the Moa

Noah the Moa lived long ago,

A very large bird as far as

birds go.

His home was New Zealand,

in the south seas, a fabulous

Janet Martin from by *Noah the Moah* ©2012

Noah the Moa

place for a moa to be.

In deep forest green Noah Moa

would roam, long before humans

came, as this was his home

and just like the kiwi this bird

Janet Martin from by *Noah the Moah* ©2012

Noah the Moa

couldn't fly, but Noah was

tall, over 3 metres high.

'How do we know about

moa?' you ask.

'How do we know moa lived

Janet Martin from by *Noah the Moah* ©2012

Noah the Moa

in the past?"

Scientists built them from bones

that were found. Discovered in

caves and dug up from the

ground.

Janet Martin from by *Noah the Moah* ©2012

The New Zealand National Anthem

God of Nations at thy feet

In the bonds of love we meet,

Hear our voices we entreat,

God defend our free land.

Guard Pacific's triple star,

T Bracken (1843-1898) from *God Defend New Zealand*

The New Zealand National Anthem

From the shafts of strife

and war,

Make her praises heard afar,

God defend New Zealand.

T Bracken (1843-1898) from God Defend New Zealand

Bound for Botany Bay

Farewell to old England forever,

Farewell to my old pals as well.

Farewell to the well-known Old Bailey,

Where I used to cut such a swell.

There's the captain who is our

commander.

Anonymous *Bound for Botany Bay*

Bound for Botany Bay

There's the bo'sun and all the

ship's crew,

There's the first and the second

class passengers,

Knows what we poor convicts

goes through.

Anonymous *Bound for Botany Bay*

Bound for Botany Bay

'Taint leaving old England we cares about.

'Taint cos we misspelt what we knows.

But because we all light-fingered gentry.

Anonymous *Bound for Botany Bay*

Bound for Botany Bay

Hops round with a log on our toes.

Now, all my young Dookies and

Duchesses,

Take warning from what I've to say—

Mind all is your own as you toucheses,

Or you'll meet us in Botany Bay.

Anonymous *Bound for Botany Bay*

Old Man Platypus

Far from the trouble and toil of town,

Where the reed-beds sweep and shiver,

Look at a fragment of velvet brown,

Old man platypus drifting down,

Drifting along the river.

And he plays and dives in the river

Banjo Patterson (1864-1941) from *Old Man Platypus*

Old Man Platypus

bends.

In a style that is most elusive,

With few relations and fewer friends,

For Old Man Platypus descends

From a family most exclusive.

He shares his burrow beneath the bank

Banjo Patterson (1864-1941) from *Old Man Platypus*

Old Man Platypus

With his wife and his son and daughter

At the roots of the reeds and the grasses

rank;

And the bubbles show where our hero

sank

To its entrance under water.

Banjo Patterson (1864-1941) from *Old Man Platypus*

Old Man Platypus

Safe in their burrow below the falls

They live in a world of wonder,

Where no one visits and no one calls,

They sleep like little brown billiard balls

With their beaks tucked neatly under.

Banjo Patterson (1864-1941) from *Old Man Platypus*

The Little Worm

Now, how does a worm loosen soil? First,

he burrows down into it—and next, he eats

large quantities of it. In these large quantities

are decaying leaves, flower petals and so on,

which are useful to him as food. The soil

itself is not needed as food, but on its way

Nuri Mass (1918-1993) from *The Wonderland of Nature* ©1964

The Little Worm

through, it is crumbled into fine pieces.

The worm then comes up and

casts it all out on the surface of

the ground — and this little mound

of digested earth is known as

'castings'. In the early morning, if

Nuri Mass (1918-1993) from *The Wonderland of Nature* ©1964

The Little Worm

you look, you will probably find

many of these castings in your

lawn and garden.

Nuri Mass (1918-1993) from *The Wonderland of Nature* ©1964

The Lizard's Boomerang

Oolah, the lizard, was tired of lying in the sun, doing nothing. So he said 'I will go and play.' He took his boomerangs out and began to practice throwing them. While he was doing so a Galah came up, and stood near

Katherine Langloh Parker (1856-1940) from *Australian Legendary Tales*

The Lizard's Boomerang

watching the boomerangs come flying

back.

...for the kind of boomerangs Oolah

was throwing were the bubberahs.

They are smaller than the others,

and more curved, and when they

Katherine Langloh Parker (1856-1940) from *Australian Legendary Tales*

The Lizard's Boomerang

are properly thrown they return

to the thrower, which other boomerangs

do not.

Katherine Langloh Parker (1856-1940) from *Australian Legendary Tales*

Bushland Stories

The wave smiled with delight, and curled over with a joyful gurgle. 'Come on, then. Come and catch me,' she called, and in a moment she was racing over the ocean with the wind behind her.

Amy Mack (1876-1939) from *Bushland Stories*

Bushland Stories

Laughing and screaming, the children

tumbled along the sand beneath her, as

she rolled them over with her arms.

She wanted to wait and play with them,

but she was moving too quickly to stop.

On she went, up the white beach.

Amy Mack (1876-1939) from *Bushland Stories*

Bushland Stories

Her heart was aching with joy.

Tenderly and softly she kissed the

sand as she passed, but each kiss

seemed to leave her weaker.

Amy Mack (1876-1939) from *Bushland Stories*

The Beach

The beach is a quarter of golden

fruit, a ripe, soft melon sliced to

a half-moon curve, having a thick

green rind of jungle growth; and the

sea devours it with its sharp, sharp,

white teeth.

William Hart Smith (1911-1990) by *The Beach*

Click Go the Shears

Out on the board the old shearer stands,

Grasping the shears in his thin, bony

hands.

Fixed is his gaze on his bare-bellied yoe,

Glory, if he gets her, won't he

make the ringer go.

Anonymous *Click Go the Shears* Australian Folk Song

Click Go the Shears

In the middle of the floor, in his cane

bottomed chair,

Sits the boss of the board with his

eyes everywhere,

Notes well each fleece as it comes to

the screen,

Anonymous *Click Go the Shears* Australian Folk Song

Click Go the Shears

Paying strict attention that it's taken

off clean.

Now Mister Newchum for to begin,

In number seven paddock bring all the

sheep in;

Don't leave none behind, whatever you

Anonymous *Click Go the Shears* Australian Folk Song

Click Go the Shears

may do,

And then you'll be fit for a jackaroo.

The tar boy is there and he's waiting

in demand,

With his blackened tar pot in his

tarry hand,

Anonymous *Click Go the Shears* Australian Folk Song

Click Go the Shears

Spies one old sheep with a cut upon

his back.

Here's what he is waiting for, it's

'Tar here, Jack.'

Click go the shears, boys,

Click, click, click.

Anonymous *Click Go the Shears* Australian Folk Song

Click Go the Shears

Wide is his blow and his hand moves quick.
The ringer looks around and he's beaten by a blow,
And curses the old snagger and the bare-bellied yoe.

Anonymous *Click Go the Shears* Australian Folk Song

Little Black Princess

Bett Bett must have been a Princess

for she was a King's niece. She

wasn't a fairy princess who waved

her golden sceptre over her subjects;

she was a little Australian Aboriginal

girl and her palace was the lonely

Adaptation from Jeannie Gunn (1870-1961) *The Little Black Princess*

Little Black Princess

Australian bush.

Bett-Bett used to help me around

the house. One of her favourite

jobs was polishing the silver,

particularly the biscuit-barrel,

which she called 'little fellow

Adaptation from Jeannie Gunn (1870-1961) *The Little Black Princess*

Little Black Princess

billy-can belonga biscuit.'

Bett Bett hated to sleep on a

mattress. 'Him too muchee jump-up

jump-up,' she would say. So she

spread out a rug on the floor and

began to jump and prance on it

Adaptation from Jeannie Gunn (1870-1961) *The Little Black Princess*

Little Black Princess

wildly. Then with her dog, two

opposums and a biscuit she snuggled

under the covers for the night.

Adaptation from *The Little Black Princess* by Mrs A Gunn © 1905

Blinky Bill

The bush was alive with

excitement. Mrs Koala had a brand

new baby, and the news had

spread like wild fire. The

kookaburras in the highest gum

trees heard of it, and laughed and

Dorothy Wall (1894-1942) from *The Complete Adventures of Blinky Bill*

Blinky Bill

chuckled at the idea.

In and out of their burrows the

rabbits came scuttling, their big

brown eyes opening wide with

wonder as they heard the news.

Over the grass the message went

Dorothy Wall (1894-1942) from *The Complete Adventures of Blinky Bill*

Blinky Bill

where Mrs Kangaroo was quietly

hopping towards her home.

She fairly leapt in the air with

joy. 'I must tell Mr Kangaroo!' she

cried and bounded away in great

hops and leaps. Even Mrs Snake,

Dorothy Wall (1894-1942) from *The Complete Adventures of Blinky Bill*

Blinky Bill

who was having a nap, awoke,

gave a wriggle, and blinked her

wicked little eyes.

The whole bushland was twittering

with the news, for a baby koala

was a great event. Mrs Koala had

Dorothy Wall (1894-1942) from *The Complete Adventures of Blinky Bill*

Blinky Bill

a baby every two years, and as

Mrs Rabbit had very, very many

during that time, you can just

imagine how surprised everyone was.

Mrs Koala nursed her baby, peeping

every now and then at the tiny creature

Dorothy Wall (1894-1942) from *The Complete Adventures of Blinky Bill*

Blinky Bill

in her pouch. This little baby was the

funniest wee creature. He was only

about an inch long and covered with

soft baby fur, had two big ears,

compared to the size of the rest of

him, a tiny black nose, and two beady eyes.

Dorothy Wall (1894-1942) from *The Complete Adventures of Blinky Bill*

Six Little New Zealanders

This was the one taunt calculated to

draw Pipi and disturb the aggravating

coolness of her temper. You see, she just

hates her name. Ngaire and Pipi are both

Maori names, and I think Ngaire rather

pretty, don't you? I like Pipi too, but it

Esther Glen (1881-1940) from *Six Little New Zealanders*

Six Little New Zealanders

always makes you think of the little

shellfish you pick up on the sand

beaches when the tides are low.

Sometimes we cook them for tea;

they're not bad, just a little like

oysters, only very, very leathery.

Esther Glen (1881-1940) from *Six Little New Zealanders*

Six Little New Zealanders

Pipi would never have them.

'Whatever did you call me after a fish for, Mother? I might just as well be Oyster or Shark or Whale.

Come to dinner, Oyster dear. Have you done your practise, Sharky love?

Esther Glen (1881-1940) from *Six Little New Zealanders*

Six Little New Zealanders

Your hair isn't brushed enough, Conger Eel. Don't eat so quickly, Cockles and Mussels. Alive, Alive Oh!' said Pipi.

Esther Glen (1881-1940) from *Six Little New Zealanders*

Farmer Shultz's Ducks

In the hills of South Australia

there is a little river with a big

name — the Onkaparinga. Once

upon a time it flowed through a

lovely valley full of apple trees

and cabbage patches, pastures and

Colin Thiele (1920-2006) from *Farmer Shultz's Ducks* ©1986

Farmer Shultz's Ducks

gardens, redgums and poplars.

In springtime there was celery on

the breath of the wind and falling

blossom like confetti on the slopes,

as if the hills were having a wedding...

All day long the ducks

Colin Thiele (1920-2006) from *Farmer Shultz's Ducks* ©1986

Farmer Shultz's Ducks

dallied by the riverside, listening

to the secrets of earth and the

words of the running water.

They could hear the grass growing

and the small seeds stretching and

the earthworms moving under the

Colin Thiele (1920-2006) from *Farmer Shultz's Ducks* ©1986

Farmer Shultz's Ducks

ground. They snoozed in the

sunshine with their heads tucked

under, or floated on the river as

softly as a blossom.

Colin Thiele (1920-2006) from *Farmer Shultz's Ducks* ©1986

A Morning Song

The thrush is in the wattle tree

And, 'Oh, you pretty dear!'

He's calling to his little wife

For all the bush to hear.

He's wanting all the bush to know

About his charming hen.

C J Dennis (1876-1938) from *A Morning Song*

A Morning Song

He sings it over fifty times,

and then begins again.

For it's Morning! Morning!

The world is wet with dew,

With tiny drops a-twinkle where the sun

comes shining through...

C J Dennis (1876-1938) from *A Morning Song*

A Morning Song

My friends are in the underbrush,

my friends are in the trees,

And merrily they welcome me with

morning melodies.

Above, below, from bush and bough each

calls his tuneful part;

C J Dennis (1876-1938) from *A Morning Song*

A Morning Song

And best of all, one trusty friend is

calling in my heart.

For it's Morning! Morning!

When night's black troubles end.

And never man was friendless yet who

stayed his own good friend.

C J Dennis (1876-1938) from A Morning Song

Donald Bradman

Donald George Bradman, nicknamed "The Don", was an Australian international cricketer, widely acknowledged as the greatest batsman of all time. Here is poem written about him at his peak.

Ding, dong, bell, Bradman made them

Author unknown *About Bradman* Published 1931

Donald Bradman

yell.

Giddy, giddy, gout, they could not

get him out.

Cry, baby bunting, the fieldsmen

gone a hunting,

Three blind mice, see how he runs.

Author Unknown *About Bradman* ©1931

Donald Bradman

Dickory, dickory, dock, he bats

round the clock.

Rock-a-bye, Bradman, on the tree top,

Here in Australia the Ashes will stop.

Bats in his finger, runs in his toes,

Bradman will lick 'em, wherever he goes.

Author Unknown *About Bradman* ©1931

Evonne Goolagong

Evonne Goolagong was from an Australian Aboriginal (Wiradjuri) family. Her father was a sheepshearer and her mother stayed home and looked after Evonne and her seven siblings.

Evonne loved tennis. At five years old.

M Morrow

Evonne Goolagong

she could be found peering through the wire of the tennis courts, watching people play.

Her first racquet was made from an old wooden fruit box. She loved to hit the ball against the wall.

M Morrow

Evonne Goolagong

After a while Evonne's skill and natural talent were obvious. When she was ten her home town thought she would win Wimbledon, they were right.

Evonne won seven Grand Slams tennis tournaments, including two Wimbledons.

Lest We Forget

Age shall not weary them,

nor the years condemn.

At the going down of the sun,

and in the morning,

We will remember them.

Lest we forget.

Laurence Binyon (1869-1943) from *For the Fallen*

Australian Bush Medicine

Our grandmother, Jaqueline, knew a lot about Bush Medicine. She used wangki (like a tomato) for sore throats and leaves of itara (river red gum) for scabies. She also used two sorts of berries, called kampurarrpa and pura, to

Mary Malbunka from *When I Was Little Like You* © 2003

Australian Bush Medicine

make people better when they were sick.

When *pipirri* (babies or children) had

mouth sores or trouble with teething, the

women used to get the bark of a tree

we call *piruwa*. They bought the bark

home with them and they cooked it in

Mary Malbunka from *When I Was Little Like You* © 2003

Australian Bush Medicine

the fire. When it was ready,

they ground the bark on the stone.

Then they put the powder on the

child's mouth. After that, the little

pipirri would get better.

Note: Some words are from Aboriginal Western Dessert Languages

Mary Malbunka from *When I Was Little Like You* © 2003

Looking For Yams

It was yam season on Cape York.

Everywhere Nyrlotte looked, yam seeds

were out. They dangled in big clumps off

vines coiled tightly around the tree.

It was a nice cool part of the afternoon.

Nyrlotte called out to her dog Stubby,

Note: Yams are similar to sweet potatoes.

Fiona Doyle from *On Country: Stories by Nyrlotte* © 2006

Looking For Yams

'Come on, boy, come with Granny and me.' Yarra birds soared lazily above. Oolai crow sleepily called out around them.

Off they went, leaving the rest of the families on the beach at Wallaby Island...

Fiona Doyle from *On Country: Stories by Nyrlotte* © 2006

Looking For Yams

Yam digging was an important time. Good yam diggers returned with lovely big healthy long ones all in one piece. Good yam diggers did not break their yams when they pulled them out.

Nyrlotte had studied granny in the past.

Fiona Doyle from *On Country: Stories by Nyrlotte* © 2006

Looking For Yams

She knew what to do once they got to their digging spot.

Fiona Doyle from *On Country: Stories by Nyrlotte* © 2006

The Star Man Comes to Visit

So the Star Man came. He brought

charts of the heavens and models of

planets and the telescope with which he

first sighted the comet, when it was no

more than a glimmer in the western sky.

And when he was done talking, he picked

Gary Crew from *Bright Star* © 1996

The Star Man Comes to Visit

up a piece of chalk just ordinary chalk

that Mr Hagley used and the boys stole

to throw at one another and turned to

the blackboard. He drew a circle, which

was the sun, and a smaller circle, which

was the earth, and then a great arch

Gary Crew from *Bright Star* © 1996

The Star Man Comes to Visit

which swept about both. 'What might this be?' he asked.

Alicia's hand shot up. "Geometry," she answered.

The Star Man Smiled. 'Indeed it is. The geometry of space.'

Gary Crew from *Bright Star* © 1996

A New Zealand Forest

In the upper North Island, where it's

moist and warm, soaring above everything

else in the forest are the majestic kauri

trees. Tane mahuta, the biggest kauri tree

in New Zealand, is also known as 'Lord

of the Forest.'

Sandra Morris from *A New Zealand Nature Journal* ©2014

A New Zealand Forest

A kauri forest is a busy place. Look

around and you will see many species of

trees, along with shrubs, ferns, grasses

and fungi. They provide a habitat for a

community of animals, birds and insects.

In this ecosystem all the plants and

Sandra Morris from *A New Zealand Nature Journal* ©2014

A New Zealand Forest

creatures depend on each other for

survival.

Native forests are a great place to make

leaf and bark rubbings. Place a piece of

paper over a tree trunk and rub gently

with a soft pencil or crayon. See how

Sandra Morris from *A New Zealand Nature Journal* ©2014

A New Zealand Forest

many different species of trees you can

make rubbings from to show contrasting

patterns and surfaces...

You can also make rubbings from leaves.

Paste the best examples into your nature

journal.

Sandra Morris from *A New Zealand Nature Journal* ©2014

The Wombat

The wombat isn't beautiful,

And hasn't any grace,

And his toes turn in when they should

turn out;

But he has an honest face.

The wombat doesn't talk much,

Launcelot Harrison (1880-1928) from *Tails and Tarradiddles*

The Wombat

But not because he can't;

He was told because he mustn't, when he

was young,

By his elderly maiden aunt.

The wombat doesn't eat much,

You'll notice as you pass;

Launcelot Harrison ((1880-1928) from *Tails and Tarradiddles*

The Wombat

For all that he wants for his supper at

night

Is a tonne or two of grass.

The wombat doesn't work much.

He only digs a hole;

But it is so wide, from side to side,

Launcelot Harrison ((1880-1928) from *Tails and Tarradiddles*

The Wombat

You'd think he digs for coal.

The wombat isn't useful,

Except for a kind of lark,

For the only thing he really has

Is to fall over in the dark.

The wombat isn't beautiful,

Launcelot Harrison ((1880-1928) from *Tails and Tarradiddles*

The Wombat

and hasn't any grace;

But I love him dearly just the same —

He's such an honest face.

Launcelot Harrison ((1880-1928) from *Tails and Tarradiddles*

Enjoyed 'Italic Print Handwriting for Kids with Downunder Classics'?

Come visit our website for more great titles.

https://myhomeschool.com

www.ingramcontent.com/pod-product-compliance
Lightning Source LLC
Chambersburg PA
CBHW042358070526
44585CB00029B/2988